FORENSIC SCIENCE INVESTIGATED

CYBERCRIME

WRITTEN BY:
Rebecca Stefoff

Marshall Cavendish
Benchmark
New York

MARSHALL CAVENDISH BENCHMARK
99 WHITE PLAINS ROAD
TARRYTOWN, NEW YORK 10591-9001
www.marshallcavendish.us

Text copyright © 2009 by Marshall Cavendish Corporation

All rights reserved. No part of this book may be reproduced or utilized in any form or by any means electronic or mechanical including photocopying, recording, or by any information storage and retrieval system, without permission from the copyright holders.

All Web sites were available and accurate when this book was sent to press.

LIBRARY OF CONGRESS CATALOGING-IN-PUBLICATION DATA
Stefoff, Rebecca, 1951-
Cybercrime / by Rebecca Stefoff.
p. cm. — (Forensic science investigated)
Includes bibliographical references and index.
ISBN 978-0-7614-3084-1
Computer crimes—Juvenile literature. 2. Forensic sciences—Juvenile literature.
I. Title.
HV6773.S734 2009
363.25'9—dc22
2008008055

EDITOR: Christina Gardeski PUBLISHER: Michelle Bisson
ART DIRECTOR: Anahid Hamparian SERIES DESIGNER: Kristen Branch

Photo Research by Anne Burns Images

Cover Photo by *Photo Researchers*/Mehau Kulyk Back Cover Photo by *Phototake*/Terry Why

The photographs in this book are used with permission and through the courtesy of: *iStockphoto*: pp. 1, 3 (hand Chris Hutchinson, cells David Marchal). *Photo Researchers*: p. 4 Bill Bachman; p. 7 Christian Darkin ; p. 51 Colin Cuthbert; p. 55 Victor Habbick Visions; p. 69 Tek Images. *Jupiter Images*: p. 12 Stock Connection. *Alamy Images*: p. 14 Sam Morgan Moore; p. 37 Eric Nathan; p. 83 K-PHOTOS. *Corbis*: p. 17 Hulton-Deutch Collection; p. 24 Lester Lefkowitz; pp. 32, 62, 66 Kim Kulish; p. 42 Jeff Christensen; p. 46 Andrew Holbrooke; p. 48 Los Angeles Daily News/Sygma; p. 53 Sion Touhig; p. 60 Reuters. *SuperStock*: p. 19 age fotostock. *Associated Press*: pp. 21, 57. *Photofest*: p. 29. *Getty Images*: p. 34 David McGlynn; p. 73 Laurence Dutton; p. 78 Louie Psihoyos.

Printed in Malaysia
1 3 5 6 4 2

Cover: The computer becomes a target for criminals.

CONTENTS

INTRODUCTION
WHAT IS FORENSICS?   4

CHAPTER ONE
THE WORLD OF HIGH-TECH CRIME   14

CHAPTER TWO
CYBERCRIMES AND CYBERCASES   34

CHAPTER THREE
COMPUTER FORENSICS   60

GLOSSARY   86
FIND OUT MORE   88
BIBLIOGRAPHY   91
INDEX   92

For millions of computer users around the world, the keyboard is the gateway to the world of cyberspace, the realm of e-mail, instant messaging, chat rooms, Web pages—and computer crime.

WHAT IS FORENSICS?

DURING THE PAST several generations, computers and the Internet have changed the world. A library's worth of knowledge can now be stored on a single hard drive small enough to fit inside a laptop computer. With a few keystrokes and mouse clicks, a woman sitting at her kitchen table in her bathrobe can shop for her child's birthday present, pay her bills, and send a memo to coworkers in her office. People on opposite sides of the world now communicate with e-mail and instant messages, share photos, collaborate on art and musical projects, and play games together. All this power and freedom, however, comes with a price: cybercrime.

Cybercrime, sometimes called computer crime, is a catchall term for any kind of wrongdoing that involves computers or the Internet. It ranges from nuisance attacks, such as vandalizing or defacing someone else's Web page, to activities with more serious or far-reaching effects, such as stalking someone in cyberspace, or launching a **virus** or **worm** that spreads through the Internet and infects millions of computers. Many computer crimes have had profound effects in the real world. Online identity theft, for example, has turned life upside down for hundreds of thousands of people. In at least one case outside the United States, a stealth Internet assault crippled whole cities with power failures.

During the 1980s and 1990s, as the Internet stitched millions of individual computers and their databases together, a new world was created. That world was cyberspace—the invisible realm of e-mails, blogs, Web pages, online shopping and game playing, and much more. Unfortunately cyberspace, like any frontier, turned out to have its share of criminals. But as each new form of computer-related crime emerged, security professionals and law enforcement agencies developed new ways of investigating, solving, and preventing such crimes. The tools and techniques they use are known as **computer forensics**, a highly specialized part of **forensic science**, which is the use of scientific methods and tools to investigate crimes.

WHAT IS FORENSICS?

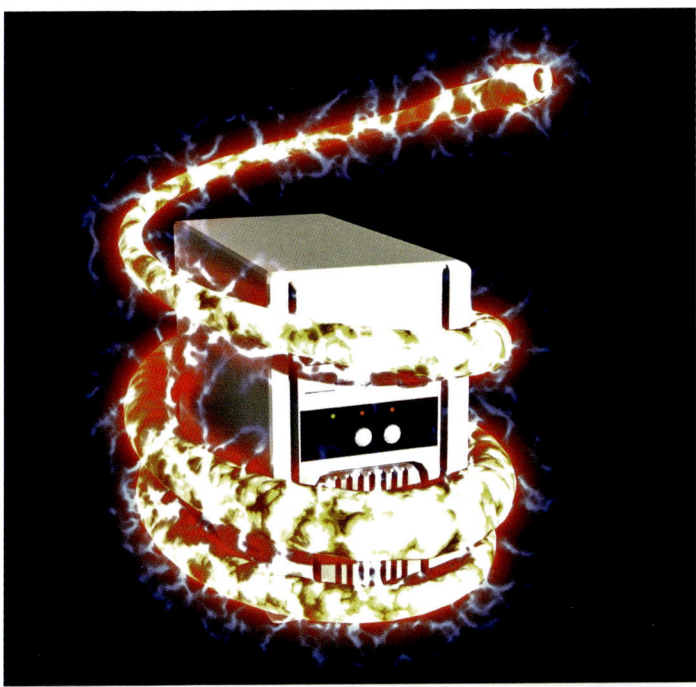

▲ A worm—symbolized here in a piece of artwork created on a computer—is a piece of malicious software code. By getting a stranglehold on many individual computers, worms create whole networks of infected machines that cybercriminals can control from a distance.

The term "forensic" comes from ancient Rome, where people debated matters of law in a public meeting place called the Forum. The Latin word *forum* gave rise to *forensic*, meaning "relating to courts of law or to public debate." Today **forensics** has several meanings. One is the art of speaking in debates, which is why some schools have forensics clubs or teams for students who want to learn debating skills. The best-known meaning of the term, though, is crime solving through forensic science.

Fascination with forensics explains the popularity of many recent TV shows, movies, and books, but crime and science have been linked for a long time. The first science used in criminal investigation was medicine, and one of the earliest reports of forensic medicine comes from ancient Rome. In 44 BCE, the Roman leader Julius Caesar was stabbed to death not far from the Forum. A physician named Antistius examined the body and found that Caesar had received twenty-three stab wounds, but only one wound was fatal.

Antistius had performed one of history's first recorded postmortem examinations, in which a physician looks at a body to find out how the person died. But forensics has always had limits. Although Antistius could point out the chest wound that had killed Caesar, he could not say who had struck the deadly blow.

Death in its many forms inspired the first forensic manuals. The oldest one was published in China in 1248. Called *Hsi duan yu* (The Washing Away of Wrongs), it tells how the bodies of people who have been strangled are different from the bodies of drowning victims. When a corpse is recovered from the water, says the manual, officers of the law should examine the tissues and small bones in the neck. Torn tissues and broken bones show that the victim met with foul play before being thrown into the water.

Poison was the subject of another landmark book in the history of forensics. In 1813 Mathieu Orfila, a professor of medical and forensic chemistry at the University of Paris, published *Traité des poisons* (A Treatise on Poisons). Orfila described the deadly effects of various mineral, vegetable, and animal substances. He laid the foundation of the modern science of toxicology, the branch of forensics that deals with poisons, drugs, and their effects on the human body.

As France's most famous expert on poisons, Orfila played a part in an 1840 criminal trial that received wide publicity. Marie LaFarge was accused of murder after her husband died. Orfila testified that he had examined the husband's corpse and found traces of arsenic. LaFarge said that she had not fed the arsenic to her husband, insisting that he must have eaten it while away from home. The court, however, sentenced her to life imprisonment. Pardoned in 1850 after ten years in prison, LaFarge died the next year, claiming innocence to the end.

The LaFarge trial and similar cases highlighted the growing use of medical evidence in criminal investigations and trials. Courts were recognizing other kinds of forensic evidence, too. In 1784 a British murder case was decided by physical evidence. The torn edge of a piece of newspaper found in the pocket of a suspect named John Toms matched the torn edge of a ball of paper found in the wound of a man killed by a pistol shot. (At the time people used rolled pieces of cloth or paper, called wadding, to hold bullets firmly in gun barrels.) Fifty-one years later, an officer of Scotland Yard, Britain's famous police division, caught a murderer by using a flaw on the fatal bullet to trace the bullet to its maker. Such cases marked the birth of ballistics, the branch of forensics that deals with firearms.

Not all forensic developments involved murder. Science was also helping to solve crimes such as arson and forgery. By the early nineteenth century, chemists had developed the first tests to identify certain dyes used in ink. Experts could then determine the age and chemical makeup of the ink on documents, such as wills and valuable manuscripts, that were suspected of being fakes.

Forensics started to become a regular part of police work at the end of the nineteenth century, after an Austrian law professor named Hans Gross published a two-volume handbook on the subject in 1893. Gross's book, usually referred to as *Criminal Investigation,* brought together all the many techniques that scientists and law enforcers had developed for examining the physical evidence of crime—bloodstains, bullets, and more. Police departments started using *Criminal Investigation* to train officers. The book entered law school courses as well.

Modern forensic experts regard Hans Gross as the founder of their profession. Among other contributions, Gross invented the word "criminalistics." He used it to refer to the general study of crime or criminals. Today the term has a narrower, more specific meaning. It refers to the study of evidence from crime scenes. In cases of cybercrime, the evidence may include not just computers, but files stored on disks or portable drives, possibly even the content of Web pages.

Almost every branch of science has been involved in criminal investigations. Meteorologists have testified about the weather on the date of a crime. Botanists have named the plants that produced tiny specks of pollen found on suspects' clothes. Dentists have matched bite marks on victims' bodies to the teeth of their killers. Anthropologists, scientists who study human beings, have helped police identify unknown corpses by supplying information about their gender, age, and ethnic background. These days software designers, computer programmers, and information technology (IT) professionals are joining the ranks of specialists whose knowledge and skills can help solve crimes.

▲ Law enforcement battles cybercrime with computer forensics. Specialists in computer hardware, software, and programming have developed tools and procedures for preparing evidence seized from computers to be presented in criminal trials.

Forensics is a vital part of modern crime solving. And, because the role of computers and the Internet in everyday life and business is likely to keep growing, computer crime is probably here to stay. So is computer forensics. When it comes to solving the crimes of the twenty-first century, the ability to crack codes and find data hidden on hard drives, or to trace computer viruses back to their creators, is as important as identifying bullets or bloodstains.

Before the days of wireless communication and cell phones, the long-distance telephone system became an illicit playground for phreakers—the forerunners of computer hackers.

CHAPTER ONE

THE WORLD OF HIGH-TECH CRIME

▼ **BEFORE PERSONAL COMPUTERS WERE**
common, before the Internet existed, there were phone **phreakers**. These were people who found ways to manipulate telephone systems illegally. Some phreakers had a simple goal: to make phone calls without paying for them. For others, though, the thrill of breaking into the system was a greater reward than any number of free calls.

The early phreakers were the forerunners of **hackers**, a term that applies to anyone who seeks unauthorized access to computers and computer networks. Although hacking is sometimes harmless—and has even been helpful on occasion—hackers have performed countless malicious or harmful acts. Criminal hacking is just one kind of illegal activity that depends on, or makes use of, computers and the Internet, two of the most widely used technological tools in the modern world.

▶ PHONE PHREAKERS AND BLUE BOXES

During the 1960s and 1970s, the only worldwide web was the telephone system. A telephone could connect a caller instantly to anyone else who had a phone, whether across the country or around the world. Telephone companies in the United States and elsewhere used a system of tones, called in-band signaling, to control the long-distance system. As users dialed numbers on their telephones, the numbers were converted into a sequences of tones. Other tones controlled certain operations within the system, such as opening a long-distance connection or indicating that a caller had hung up. Phreaking was born when a few people discovered that by duplicating those tones, they could trick the system.

A few of the early phreakers were blind people, some of them kids or teenagers, who had developed unusual sensitivity to sound. They were able to memorize the tones they heard over the telephone lines and reproduce them by whistling. Others were students who found details about in-band signaling, including

THE WORLD OF HIGH-TECH CRIME

▲ In 1971, when this photo was taken, some telephone systems still had manual switchboards, with operators connecting long-distance calls. But direct-dialing, which let phone users place the calls themselves, was on the rise, and some users had figured out how to trick its signaling system.

the exact frequencies for various tones, in articles published in technical journals by AT&T, the company that controlled the American telephone system at the time. This information made it possible for anyone with just a bit of engineering skill to create a small device called a multifrequency tone generator that could be used to manipulate the phone system. Soon nicknamed blue boxes, these little gadgets let users hijack a phone line and call anyone, anywhere, at no cost.

Getting free calls was only part of the fun. Phreakers reveled in exploring the "landscape" of the telephone system, figuring out how the parts of the system were interconnected and how things worked. They staged elaborate stunts in which they routed a free call around the world, trying to pass through the phone systems of as many nations as possible, only to finish by making a phone ring in the same room where the call had originated.

In 1971, *Esquire* magazine published an article titled "Secrets of the Little Blue Box" that introduced phreaking to the general public. The following year *Ramparts* magazine published instructions for building a multifrequency tone generator. Although the phone company successfully sued *Ramparts* and forced it to destroy many copies of the magazine, and although some phreakers were arrested and convicted for theft of phone services, by that time the phreaking subculture was well established.

▶ FROM PHREAKING TO HACKING

During the 1980s, personal computers came into use and the early Internet took shape. Then, in the 1990s, the World Wide Web—the set of graphic images and pages that makes up most people's experience of the Internet—developed. During these decades some

THE WORLD OF HIGH-TECH CRIME

▲ The World Wide Web connected people around the globe as never before. It also opened up new opportunities for mischief and mayhem.

phreakers turned their attention to computers and began hacking large computer systems, including the computer systems of telephone companies. Among them were members of a notorious phreaker group that called itself the Legion of Doom, after a comic-book cluster of supervillains. One member of this

CAPTAIN CRUNCH

JOHN DRAPER WAS an Air Force veteran and engineering student in California during the early 1970s, when he became known in the phreaker subculture by his chosen handle, Captain Crunch. The name referred to Cap'n Crunch, a cereal brand that became popular with phreakers. For a time, the manufacturer of Cap'n Crunch included toy whistles in boxes of the cereal. Phreakers had found that if one of the holes in the whistle was plugged by glue, the toy emitted a tone at the frequency 2,600 hertz (Hz)—exactly the frequency needed to open switches in the telephone system.

Draper was one of several phreakers who were profiled in the widely read 1971 article about blue boxes in *Esquire* magazine. After the article appeared, the FBI took an interest in phreakers, including Captain Crunch. In 1972 Draper was convicted on a federal charge, the fraudulent theft of toll services. It was the first of his three convictions for phone fraud during the 1970s.

Yet Draper is also recognized as a pioneering figure in the history of Silicon Valley, the area near San Francisco where many computer and Internet companies originated. He knew Steve Wozniak and Steve Jobs, the founders of the Apple computer company, and spent several stints as an Apple employee. Among other contributions to early computing technology, Draper developed equipment that was eventually used in voice-activated phone menus

JOHN DRAPER IN 1978, AFTER NEARLY A DECADE AS A LEGENDARY PHONE PHREAKER.

and voice mail messaging. He also wrote a software program called EasyWriter that was used in computers manufactured by both Apple and IBM, which was then the leading maker of PCs. More recently, Draper has designed computer security equipment. Success in business has eluded Captain Crunch, however, perhaps because his criminal record unsettles some potential employers, investors, and clients.

During one stretch in a minimum-security prison, Draper protected himself from mistreatment by other inmates by teaching them phreaking skills. He held informal classes in which he showed fellow inmates how to build blue boxes, how to prevent their calls from being tapped or traced, and how to make pagers out of old radios. "Prisons," Draper now declares on his Web site, "are universities of crime."

As for Draper's reasons for phreaking the phone system, he said in the *Esquire* article, "If I do what I do, it is only to explore a system." One of the judges who sentenced Captain Crunch saw things differently. "You have to pay for your long-distance phone calls," the judge told Draper. "Is that such a very difficult moral concept to grasp?" Visionary explorers or simple lawbreakers? Phreakers and hackers like Captain Crunch have been seen as both.

phreaker-hacker community, a young man named Corey Lindsly, went on to become the ringleader of the Phonemasters, a hacker gang that made cybercrime history in the 1990s.

LISTENING IN

From the point of view of law enforcement, the Phonemasters case began in the summer of 1994, when the FBI office in Dallas, Texas, received a call from a local private investigator (PI). The PI told authorities that a young man named Calvin Cantrell had offered to sell him personal information—private phone numbers, credit reports, and more—for any individual he named. The FBI asked the PI to wear a wire, or concealed microphone, and record further conversations with Cantrell. The PI agreed, and the conversations contained so much incriminating material that the FBI was able to obtain a warrant to tap Cantrell's phone line.

The telephone wiretap let the authorities eavesdrop on their suspect's spoken conversations, but what really interested Michael Morris, an FBI computer expert, was that Cantrell was spending as many as fifteen hours a day connected by phone to telecommunications companies such as Sprint, General Telephone and Electronics (GTE), and Southwestern Bell. These were not voice communications. Instead, Cantrell was linking to the corporate phone systems through a dial-up Internet connection. To discover what Cantrell was up to during those hours, Morris needed a way to tap into the data that was traveling in and out of Cantrell's modem, the part of his computer that translated data from the **digital** form used by the computer into signals that could be carried along the phone line, and vice versa. No reliable data-tapping device existed at the time, but the FBI was developing one.

DATA TAPPING

After discussions with the U.S. Department of Justice, Morris received the first permit for data tapping ever issued by the federal government. In December 1994 the newly completed data-tapping device was installed in a warehouse that stood between Cantrell's home and the telephone company office where his calls were processed. The device intercepted and interpreted the data that passed along Cantrell's telephone line, translating the whine of the modem's signal into a digital record of the keystrokes Cantrell made on his keyboard. The agents assigned to monitor the device soon discovered that Cantrell was not operating alone. He was part of an eleven-person ring that the FBI eventually nicknamed the Phonemasters because they were so good at sneaking into telephone systems.

▲ The Phonemasters used telephone lines to break into companies' computer systems and steal data. By tapping into one of those phone lines, the FBI gathered evidence against the Phonemasters.

In 1994, cell phone use was not as widespread as it now is. Most people used pay phones and other land-line phones to make their long-distance calls, charging the calls to their calling card numbers, which were special numbers that individual customers could use to make long-distance calls from any telephone. The Phonemasters' main business activity was to exploit security gaps in the telephone companies' systems by hacking into the companies' databases to get customers' calling card numbers. The gang sold these numbers to people who used them to make free calls.

The original customers were billed for the stolen calls, but in most cases, once they protested the charges, they were excused from paying them. The telecommunications companies absorbed the cost, so they, not the customers, were the victims. Ultimately, the hackers' activities would cost the telecom companies almost $2 million. Although this amount was not large to companies that routinely dealt in tens or hundreds of millions of dollars, the thefts revealed security weaknesses that could have resulted in much more serious losses.

The Phonemasters also hacked into phone directories at the FBI and other organizations and sold the numbers to foreign businesses, which charged their customers' calls to the stolen numbers. As a result, the FBI and other organizations were billed for hundreds of thousands of dollars' worth of calls their employees did not make. In addition, by hacking into the databases of major financial companies, such as the credit-reporting firm Equifax, the Phonemasters were able to harvest people's personal information, including Social Security numbers and credit card numbers. They sold this information, which the buyers could use to commit fraud or identity theft.

BUSTED

As the FBI agents monitored Cantrell's phone calls and online activities, they realized that the Phonemasters' leader was Corey Lindsly, a student at the University of Pennsylvania. Lindsly was no stranger to hacking. In 1989, at the age of twenty-two, he had pled guilty in an Oregon court to using a computer to break into the US West telephone system. Perhaps Lindsly knew that the Phonemasters were bound to get caught. He warned his fellow hackers in January 1995, "We're all gonna get busted anyway." A few weeks later, with evidence in hand, the FBI shut down the Phonemasters, arresting Lindsly, Cantrell, and other members of the group.

After pleading guilty to criminal fraud and illegal use of access devices and computers, Lindsly and others received fines and prison sentences. As the group's ringleader, Lindsly received a sentence of forty-one months in prison. When the sentence was handed down in 1999, it was the second-longest sentence that had been given for hacking.

The Phonemasters case contained elements of both phreaking and hacking, and since the 1990s the two activities have become even more closely intertwined. These days, phreaking is generally a form of hacking, because phone systems are now controlled by computers. Both telephones and computers increasingly use wireless methods of communication, and telephone systems rely on digital signals rather than tones.

▶ WHO HACKS, AND WHY?

The Phonemasters were nothing more than a criminal syndicate, hacking for profit. Other hackers, though, viewed themselves and their activities in a different light. They considered themselves to be rebel geniuses on the fringes of mainstream society, creative explorers of new electronic frontiers.

In 1986 a member of the Legion of Doom released a document known as both "The Conscience of a Hacker" and "The Hacker Manifesto." It sets forth the image of the hacker as one who defies law and government for noble reasons:

> This is our world now . . . the world of the electron and the switch . . . . We make use of a

service already existing without paying for what could be dirt-cheap if it wasn't run by profiteering gluttons, and you call us criminals. We explore . . . and you call us criminals. We seek after knowledge . . . and you call us criminals. We exist without skin color, without nationality, without religious bias . . . and you call us criminals. You build atomic bombs, you wage wars, you murder, cheat and lie to us and try to make us believe it's for our own good, yet we're the criminals.

Movies such as *War Games* (1983) and *Hackers* (1995), as well as many TV shows and graphic novels, helped to spread the idea that at least some hackers are underground heroes. One reason this image of hackers is attractive is that many people like the idea that brains and computing skill, rather than muscle and fighting ability, can save the day—or the world. At the same time, though, another media image of hackers arose, one that portrayed the hacker as juvenile and socially backward. Law enforcement and computer security agencies have learned, meanwhile, that many hackers are simply career criminals who have found the Internet to be a profitable place to commit crimes. The truth is that there is no "typical" hacker—they are a highly diverse bunch.

THE WORLD OF HIGH-TECH CRIME | 29

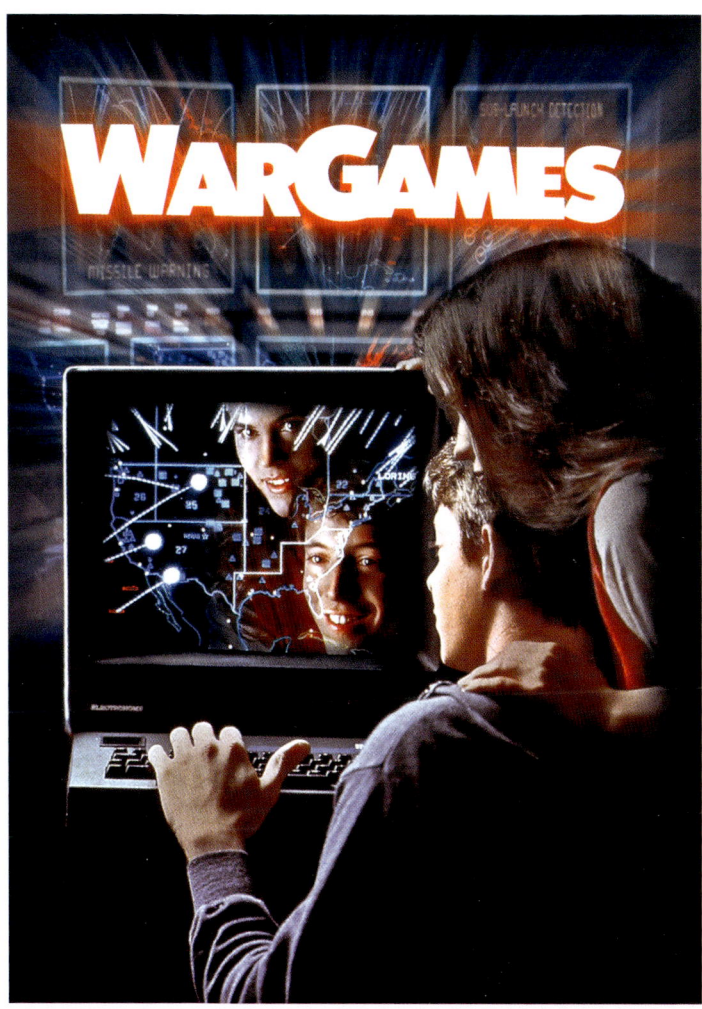

▲ *War Games*, a 1983 movie starring Mathew Broderick and Ally Sheedy, is the story of a young computer genius who hacks into a top-secret military supercomputer and almost starts World War III by accident.

Hackers' motives and activities are diverse, too, and this has given rise to a vocabulary for various kinds of hacking. People who hack for criminal or malicious purposes are called black hats or **crackers**. Those who sell stolen or pirated software or files are known as wares dudes—or, in the style of hackers, online gamers, and other computer users who adopt distinctive spellings and replace letters with numbers, warez d00dz. Activists who hack for political reasons or to advance a cause—perhaps vandalizing the Web sites of politicians or corporations they oppose, or inserting slogans such as "End animal testing now" into other people's Web sites—call themselves hacktivists.

Script kiddies are relatively unskilled hackers who use commonly available hacking tools rather than creating their own. Their goal is generally to create havoc and seize control of systems. More skilled hackers, in contrast, often try to work stealthily, in such a way that their activities go unnoticed. Such hackers are sometimes tolerated or even hired by organizations to probe for weaknesses in computer security. In this role they may be called sneakers.

The line between "outlaw" hackers and the "establishment" is often blurry. Some hackers have worked for or sold their consulting services to the very institutions whose systems they have hacked. At hacker events such as DEF CON, an annual convention in Las Vegas, representatives from private businesses and the federal government have recruited promising hackers to work for them. (One feature of the convention is the "spot the fed" contest, in which hackers in attendance win T-shirts for identifying federal representatives who are hoping to pass unnoticed among them.)

White hats are people who hack for so-called good reasons, such as the pursuit of knowledge, the pleasure of solving problems, or the testing and improvement of computer security. In August 2007, for example, an Australian teenager named Tom Wood hacked a piece of software that his country's government had spent $84 million to acquire. Designed to protect children from Internet pornography, the filter had been made available for free to any family that wanted to download it.

After downloading the filter "to see how good it was," Wood cracked it in about half an hour. Wood, who has campaigned for cybersafety for children, told reporters that the filter represented "a horrible waste of money." He claimed that parents and the government should be aware that kids with computer skills might be able to bypass the filter, leaving their parents none the wiser.

Wood's act qualifies as hacking because he had deliberately set out to "break" a piece of software. Yet the act did not enable him to commit fraud, steal

▲ In DEF CON's Capture the Flag contest, teams of hackers spend several days defending their own computers or networks while attacking those of rival teams.

money, or purloin confidential information. Wood believed he was performing a public service by hacking the filter and making a public statement about it. Critics pointed out, on the other hand, that Wood's announcement might simply inspire other young people to hack the filter that was supposed to protect them. Was Wood's hacking stunt helpful or harmful?

There may be no simple answer. A similar stunt performed on a bank's electronic security system, however, would clearly be a criminal act.

People who hack in both helpful and harmful ways are sometimes called gray hats. They may serve as watchdogs, exposing the weaknesses in software and computer systems, yet they also commit computer crimes, such as obtaining free phone calls or defacing Web sites. The idea that hacking can sometimes be a good thing is reflected in popular entertainment, which has many appealing hacker characters. In reality, though, hacking is an illegal activity with enormous potential for harm to individuals, businesses, and government. The out-and-out criminals known as black hat hackers contribute to the ever-growing problem of computer crime.

The crime scene is a computer's hard drive in many twenty-first-century criminal investigations.

CHAPTER TWO

CYBERCRIMES AND CYBERCASES

▼ **HACKING, WHICH IS ITSELF UNLAWFUL,** plays a key role in many other kinds of cybercrimes. Yet not all computer-related crimes involve hacking. Many forms of criminal activity involve computers—so many that some law enforcement experts divide computer crime into categories. Marjie T. Britz, author of *Computer Forensics and Cyber Crime: An Introduction* (2004), recognizes three categories, based on the different roles that computers play in crime. Computers may be incidental to crime, they may be the tools or means of committing crime, or they may be the targets of crime.

▶ COMPUTERS AS INCIDENTAL

A computer is incidental to a crime when it is present or involved in some way, without being used in committing the crime. Evidence related to a robbery or murder, for example, might be contained in documents or e-mails stored on a suspect's computer. Goods stolen in a household or business burglary might include a computer or computers. Although law enforcement does not regard such cases as cybercrimes, whenever computers or computer files are part of the evidence in any crime, they require proper handling according to the techniques of computer forensics, so that both the computers and any evidence they contain will be protected.

▶ COMPUTERS AS TOOLS

A vast array of crimes that can be committed without computers may be easier to commit with the help of computers. Identity thieves, for example, can gather personal information the old-fashioned way, such as by sifting through people's trash for their bank account or credit card numbers. Or they can use computers as tools, hacking into the databases of financial companies and illegally copying the desired information.

The same thing applies to many other crimes, such as stalking. In the physical world, stalking might mean following someone or making repeated, unwelcome phone calls or visits. Cyberstalking, which is illegal in the United States, involves such tactics as posting false or negative information about the victim on Web pages, defacing the victim's own Web pages, gathering information about the victim from online sources, posting the victim's address and telephone number online and encouraging other people to harass the victim, bombarding the victim with **spam** (junk or unwanted e-mail), hacking into the victim's own e-mail account and sending offensive e-mails that appear to be from the victim, and trying to lure the victim into a real-life meeting.

▲ The all-too-familiar clutter in an e-mail inbox is more than an irritation. Such e-mails can lure readers into becoming victims of fraud or identity theft.

Computers have made some crimes easier than ever. For example, the invention of e-mail has vastly increased the scope of certain types of fraud that were once carried out by written mail. One of the most widely used frauds, known to law enforcement as the 419 or Nigerian fee scheme, starts with an e-mail supposedly from a highly placed person, often a banker or government official in the African nation of Nigeria. The writer of the e-mail claims to have access to a large sum of money—usually in the millions of dollars—and offers to share it with the person who received the e-mail. All the lucky recipient has to do to get his or her hands on part of the fortune is send the letter writer a sum of money in advance to cover official fees, bribes, or the cost of transferring the fortune to the recipient's bank account.

No one who has ever responded to such an offer, it is safe to say, received the fortune that was promised. Sadly, many people have lost thousands of dollars to this and similar schemes. Most good e-mail programs now block or flag this particular form of spam, but other fraudulent offers may slip through. Anyone who uses an e-mail account should remember that if an offer looks too good to be true, it is not true. Computer security experts say that if you receive an e-mail that offers to give or sell you something, the smartest thing to do is delete it—without opening it, if possible, and definitely without replying to it.

Phishing is an attempt to steal confidential information by sending an e-mail that appears to be from a trusted source—a bank, for example, or a major corporation such as Microsoft, or an e-commerce site such as eBay. The recipient is asked to click on a link in order to be taken to a secure site where he or she will be asked to provide, verify, or change information such as a password, user ID, or account number. In reality, the link takes the recipient to the phisher's site, where the information is harvested for sale and possible use in fraud or identity theft. Again, the best defense against phishing is caution. Instead of clicking on a link in an e-mail, use your Internet browser to go to the main Web site of the company that supposedly sent you the e-mail, and then tell the organization's customer service department about the e-mail. Banks and other legitimate businesses never ask for confidential information by e-mail.

Stealing by someone in a position of trust, such as an employee or a manager of funds, is known as embezzlement. In earlier times, embezzlement involved such activities as stealing money from the company safe or cash drawer, or manipulating the account books. Today computerized banking, bookkeeping, and money transferring have made new forms of embezzlement possible. One type of embezzlement is called the salami scheme because it involves stealing money in many tiny "slices," like thin pieces cut from a salami. In this scheme, the embezzler uses specially created software programs to shave off tiny amounts of money, such as thousandths or even ten-thousandths of a cent, and deposit them in a secret account belonging to the embezzler. A ten-thousandth of a penny may not sound like much, but if the embezzler's institution handles thousands or even millions of accounts, those fractions add up over time to a substantial sum.

Another crime that has migrated to cyberspace is extortion, which is a demand for money, backed up by threats to harm the victim unless the payment is made. "Protection," in which store owners pay local thugs or gangsters to prevent "accidents" such as broken windows or beatings, is a traditional urban extortion racket. In the twenty-first century, some extortionists are hackers who have penetrated the computer systems of large corporations. The hacker threatens to reveal to the public that the system has been hacked unless the company makes a payment. Some firms give in to the demand because such an announcement would cause customers to lose confidence in the company, resulting in loss of business.

Details about cyberextortion are scarce, because companies and businesses that have been hacked generally want to keep their misfortune secret. For this reason they often fail to report extortion to law enforcement. According to observers of cybercrime trends such as Alan Paller, research director at a computer security firm called SANS, the victims of cyberextortion have included online shopping sites, online gambling sites, and banks. These victims have been willing to pay, both to keep their sites from being shut down by hackers and to keep the hackers from going public with their exploits.

The distribution of child pornography is one of the most widespread and disturbing cybercrimes. Statistics on Internet pornography are highly variable, but after surveying information published by several dozen newspapers, government agencies, and research groups, an organization called Internet Filter Review claimed that in 2006 as many as 100,000 Web sites offered pornographic materials featuring children. Making, distributing, and downloading sexual images of children is illegal. So is "trolling," or using the Internet to search for young people with the goal of making them victims of sex crimes. Identifying and prosecuting people guilty of these acts is one of the most active areas of cybercrime investigation.

Some crimes can be committed only with the help of computers, the Internet, or other high-technology communications tools. One such crime is digital piracy, the illegal copying or downloading of copyrighted material, such as music and films, in digital form. The crime is the unlicensed use of the copyrighted material, which could not have taken place without the means of transmitting and storing the data. High-speed Internet connections and media software have made it

▲ Invented by college student Shawn Fanning, Napster started as a free program for sharing music files. After a court order shut down Napster, the name was bought by a legal, pay-for-tunes service.

technically simple for individuals to share music and video files, but such activities are risky. Industry groups such as the Motion Picture Association of America (MPAA) and the Recording Industry Association of America (RIAA), as well as studios and companies that own the copyrighted material, have sued both file-sharing sites, such as Napster, and individuals who have downloaded unlicensed material.

▶ COMPUTERS AS TARGETS

Many cybercrimes are aimed at computers themselves. These crimes take place in the physical world as well as in cyberspace. Theft of computer software and hardware, especially small but costly elements such as microprocessor chips and memory cards, ranges from individual cases of pilfering to large-scale enterprises. In February 2001, for example, the FBI arrested two employees of a company that provides call-center services for other companies. The men had used their employer's computer system to send nearly three-quarters of a million dollars' worth of computer products to places where the schemers could collect them for resale on the black market. Such crimes may have an international dimension, because computer materials that are considered out of date in North America and Japan remain desirable and valuable in other parts of the world.

PIRACY

Software piracy covers a wide range of activities, but in each case the crime is the theft or unlicensed use of a software program. Often the criminals are individual users who purchase popular programs such as Microsoft Office and then pass out copies to family and friends. Others "borrow" software paid for by their employers and use it on their home computers.

Some illicit users may not realize that they have broken the law. The purchaser of a computer disk containing a software program does not really own the program, however. Instead, the purchaser becomes a licensed user whose right to copy the program is strictly limited by law.

Large-scale, organized software piracy generally involves copying or counterfeiting programs and selling them as original. In the summer of 2001, after an investigation that had lasted longer than a year, FBI agents arrested four men with more than $10 million worth of counterfeit Microsoft software.

HACK ATTACKS

Hacking is a direct attack on a specific computer or computer network. It sometimes occurs through the keyboard—in other words, the hacker sits down in front of the target computer, possibly belonging to a friend, family member, school, or library that makes computers available for public use, and tries to gain access to its operating system by means of keyboard commands. The great majority of hacking attacks, however, are remote, which means that the hacker uses his or her own computer to attack another computer over the Internet or over a telephone connection. The hacker and the target may be in adjoining rooms or on different continents.

One form of hacking is the denial of service (DoS) attack, usually aimed at large computer networks. In these attacks, the hacker is not necessarily interested in gaining access to the target computer network. The goal is to shut down a Web site or network by overloading it, usually by swamping it with e-mails or hidden code produced by automated programs. When the target is overloaded, customers or users who try to visit the site or use the network cannot do so. They are denied service.

DoS attacks have shut down major Internet sites for periods ranging from minutes to hours. In February 2000, for example, a series of attacks paralyzed some of the Internet's busiest and most popular sites, including amazon.com, yahoo.com, ebay.com, cnn.com, and several social networking sites. The culprit was a Canadian teenager who used the hacker name Mafiaboy.

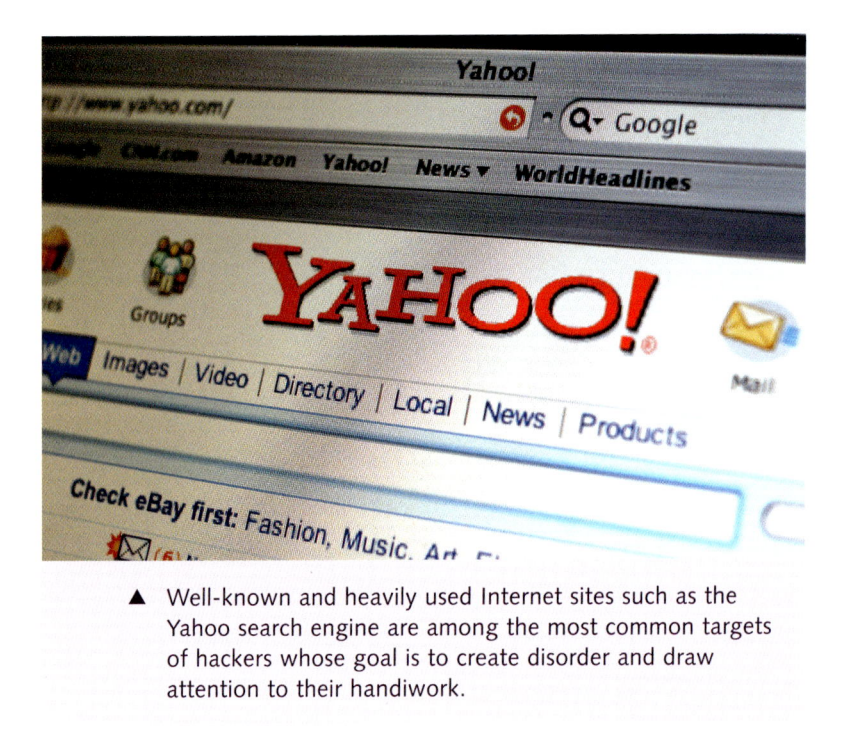

▲ Well-known and heavily used Internet sites such as the Yahoo search engine are among the most common targets of hackers whose goal is to create disorder and draw attention to their handiwork.

Authorities caught him after he boasted on several public Internet sites that he had hacked CNN.com. He was fined and sentenced to eight months in a juvenile detention facility and a year of probation.

WEB WAR I

Although large-scale DoS attacks have resulted in commercial losses due to lost business, organized DoS assaults on national infrastructures—services such as power companies, air traffic control systems, and military and telecommunications networks—could have deadly results. Estonia, a small country on the coast of the Baltic Sea in northern Europe, had a frightening lesson in the perils of DoS attacks in April 2007. Over a period of about three weeks, floods of junk messages clogged key Estonian Web sites, including those of the nation's parliament, president, prime minister, and biggest bank, as well as newspapers and other services. Hackers also vandalized the site of one political party, adding a fraudulent message to the site. With the help of computer security experts and Internet managers from around the world, Estonian IT workers gradually blocked the attacks and returned their nation's Internet sites to normal.

"Web War I" is how some observers described the attack on Estonia. Officials in the Baltic nation blamed the data flood on their neighbor to the east, Russia, but the identity of the hacker or hackers behind the attack is unknown. Other notorious hackers, however, have been identified and charged with crimes. While cyberhistorians disagree about who was the most notorious hacker of all time, they agree that Kevin Mitnick made hacker history.

A HISTORIC HACKER

Mitnick, born in 1963, was a phonc phreaker in high school. His first conviction for hacking came in 1983, when the Internet as we know it today did not yet exist.

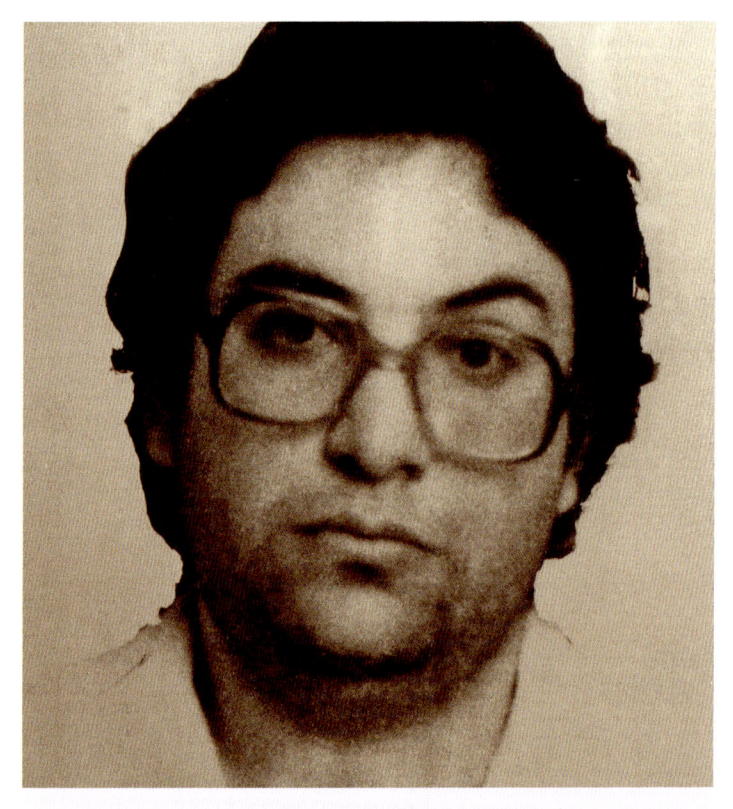

▲ Kevin Mitnick, shown here in a 1989 photograph, was one of the first computer criminals known to the general public. Exaggerated rumors credited Mitnick with mythical exploits such as hacking into defense networks that control nuclear weapons.

Mitnick was convicted of hacking into ARPANET, an early computer network created by the U.S. Department of Defense that is regarded as the forerunner of the Internet. Later in the 1980s Mitnick received several convictions for hacking and for stealing software. He was placed on probation but went underground in 1992. After several years as a fugitive, he was arrested in 1995. Mitnick served five years in prison and an additional three on parole. The computer companies from which he stole software have estimated that he cost them a total of more than $291 million.

Kevin Mitnick, who now runs his own computer security business, embodies the dual nature of some hackers, as well as the different attitudes people hold toward hackers and their activities. Mitnick described himself as an electronic joyrider, a trespasser rather than a thief, and to some he became an underground cyberhero. To others, such as the U.S. government and Tsutomu Shimomura, a scientist whose computer Mitnick hacked, he was simply a lawbreaker. Reactions to Mitnick remain mixed today. In 2006 his own Web sites were repeatedly defaced by hackers—and then repaired by other hackers.

▶ THE THREAT OF CYBERTERRORISM

Could an attack over the Internet cripple whole cities? According to the U.S. Central Intelligence Agency (CIA), it already has. Attackers have hacked into the computer systems of utility companies in other countries, according to Tom Donahue, head of computer security analysis for the agency. In one case the attack led to a power failure in multiple cities.

Although the CIA did not say which foreign cities were affected, or when the attack occurred, in January 2008 Donahue warned the heads of security for several hundred American electric, water, oil, and gas companies that their facilities might be at risk of similar attacks. Computerized systems now control many of the switches, valves, and other equipment used to operate dams, power plants, oil pipelines, railroads, and similar facilities. Terrorists attacking these systems through the Internet could cause untold damage. The Federal Energy Regulation Commission responded to Donahue's warning by issuing eight new security standards for electric utility companies, including improved security training and physical protection of vital computer equipment.

The U.S. government recognizes that cyberterrorism, like other forms of terrorism, is a threat to national security. The Department of Homeland Security (DHS) operates the National Cyber Security Division (NCSD), which coordinates efforts to prevent cyberthreats to the nation's infrastructure. In February 2006 the NCSD carried out a training exercise called Cyber Storm, which involved more than one hundred organizations in sixty locations and five countries.

▲ Mainframes, such as these machines at a water utility company, are large computers used for complex data-processing tasks. Terrorist attacks on such systems could cripple vital services in a city, region, or entire nation.

Cyber Storm imitated an attack by hackers and cyberterrorists on America's energy, telecommunications, IT, and transportation industries.

The purpose of Cyber Storm was to see how well security officers, law enforcement personnel, and government agencies responded to a crisis. On the whole, participating groups reacted quickly to the fast-moving

Cyber Command

THE U.S. AIR FORCE (USAF) is preparing to fight the nation's battles on electronic battlefields. Michael Wynne, secretary of the Air Force, declared in 2005 that the service would soon be ready to "fly and fight in air, space, and cyberspace." In early 2008 a new branch of the USAF was born. Known as Air Force Cyber Command (AFCYBER), the new command will coordinate training and programs to defend American military computer networks from hacking and other attacks—and also to attack the computer networks of terrorists or nations with which the United States might find itself at war.

The location of AFCYBER's headquarters has not yet been determined. Neither has the total number of service people and officers who will be assigned to the new command. In December 2007, however, the first group of USAF cyberwarriors graduated from a training program that is expected to produce about one hundred graduates each year. "Tell the nation," USAF secretary Wynne declared when the group began its training, "that the age of cyberwarfare is here."

. . . . .

series of simulated disasters, but they did not always communicate effectively with each other or with the media. Some responders, overwhelmed with specific crises, were slow to piece together the big picture of the overall attack. The NCSD may hold another national cyberterrorism exercise, but in the meantime it oversees programs aimed at protecting the national infrastructure from cyberterrorism while also preparing the best possible response to such an attack.

▶ **MALICIOUS SOFTWARE**

Computers and networks are vulnerable to more than hacking. They are also subject to indirect attacks by **malware**, or "malicious software." Malware is any piece

▲ An antivirus program has identified and isolated e-mails containing the ILOVEYOU worm (also known as the Love Bug), which first attacked computers on May 4, 2000.

of programming that can spread from computer to computer and has a destructive or unwanted effect on the computers it infects. There are several kinds of malware. Depending on the intentions of their creators, they can produce a wide variety of effects.

Viruses were the first form of malware to become a problem for Internet users. A virus is a piece of software code that can replicate, or create copies of, itself. It travels between computers by attaching itself to a host, such as a computer file or disk. Viruses today are most often spread in the form of e-mail attachments or "free" downloads such as screen savers and icons. In addition to the ability to replicate, a virus carries a payload of code that becomes active once the virus has infected a new computer. The payload might destroy files in the infected computer, prevent the user from connecting to the Internet, or otherwise downgrade the infected computer.

A worm is another type of malware that can replicate itself. Unlike a virus, a worm does not require a host. Worms can spread themselves independently through network or Internet connections, often by e-mailing copies of themselves to every contact in an e-mail program's address book. Worms can take up so much storage space and computing power that the computer's operating system crashes.

▲ An artist's impression of computer worms, which reproduce quickly and spread from a single computer. By taking up bandwidth, or electronic operating "space," worm attacks can slow the Internet around the world.

The first major worm attack on the Internet took place in 1988, when a Cornell University student named Robert Tappan Morris wrote a piece of code and turned it loose in cyberspace. The Morris worm is also known as the Great Worm, a reference to the scale of damage and upheaval it caused.

Morris claimed that he had not set out to cripple the Internet—he had merely wanted to see how far his worm could spread itself, and whether he could use it to measure the size of the Internet. A flaw in his code, however, caused the worm to spread differently than he had expected. Although Morris had not intended for any single computer to receive more than one copy of the worm, the worm infected computers and networks multiple times, clogging and crashing them. The Internet was young at the time, with perhaps as few as 60,000 computers connected to it. As many as a tenth of them were infected with the Great Worm. Estimates of the dollar value of the damage have ranged from $5 million to $100 million.

The Morris worm had consequences for its creator and for the Internet. Charged with violations of a federal law called the Computer Fraud and Abuse Act (CFAA), Morris was fined and sentenced to 400 hours of community service and three years' probation. (Morris later became a professor at the Massachusetts Institute of Technology. His father, also a computer scientist, was one of the experts at the National Security Agency who helped battle the Great Worm.) In response to the disaster of the Great Worm, computer experts from universities, private firms, and government agencies formed the Computer Emergency Response Team (CERT). Today known as the U.S. Computer Emergency Readiness Team (US-CERT), this organization operates through the Department of Homeland Security and releases security updates on viruses, worms, and other cyberthreats.

CYBERCRIMES AND CYBERCASES

▲ Journalists clamor for a comment from Robert Tappan Morris, whose misguided attempt to measure the size of the Internet resulted in a computer disaster known as the Great Worm.

Worms and other forms of malware may make multiple appearances. Hackers often study and copy virus or worm code, then reissue it in slightly altered form. The Storm worm, for example, first appeared in early 2007, carried by spam e-mails with subject lines that sounded like news headlines. A year later it reappeared, this time in e-mails that looked like Valentine's Day messages, with subject lines such as "Sending You My Love." The e-mail messages contain offers that sound attractive: links to greeting cards from friends or romantic cards from secret admirers, or to free games or music by top performers. Unwary users who click on these links, however, download **Trojan horses** into their computers.

A Trojan horse is a malware program that is designed to look like an ordinary file or picture—something that unsuspecting users will allow into their computers. Embedded in the Trojan horse, however, is hidden code that will carry out the hacker's purpose. Many Trojan horses create what hackers call a back door, which is a concealed hole in the computer's programming that can allow hackers to gain entry. The Trojan horse spread by the Storm worm turns the infected computer into a bot—a zombie or slave computer—that can be ordered to perform secret tasks without a user's knowledge. Such tasks might include gathering information on the user or sending e-mails as part of a DoS attack.

In December 2007 Internet security analysts for the technology company Cisco Systems predicted that the botnet, or zombie network of infected computers, created by the Storm worm will be rented out to cybercriminals for use in spam, scam, or DoS attacks. A few weeks later, IT experts around the world reported on the troubling rise of a new worm, Nugache, that seems designed to create another criminal botnet-for-hire. The Cisco statement also echoed other reports that show that cybercrime is no longer the territory of the lone hacker.

Organized crime syndicates in Russia and elsewhere are becoming ever more deeply involved in online crime.

Lone hackers, however, are still responsible for most software bombs. This type of hidden malware can lie concealed amid ordinary programming. A time bomb is set to go off at a predetermined time, while a logic bomb is set to go off when a particular event takes place. People have embedded logic bombs in their employers' computer systems, designed to damage or destroy the company's files as an act of revenge if the employee is fired. Such a bomb might be triggered by the removal of the employee's name from the payroll list.

Traditionally, creators of malware have gained no profit from their creations. Although some have claimed that they released their viruses and worms to teach computer users the importance of good security, a more common motive is probably to get attention and see how far their work will spread. Profit, however, is surely a motive behind the creation of malware-for-hire such as the Storm botnet.

New malware creations, as well as other forms of cyber mayhem, appear all the time. To investigate these computer-related crimes, security professionals and law enforcement personnel rely on the tools and techniques of computer forensics.

A technician at the German data-recovery firm Convar examines a damaged computer hard drive. Using a laser scanning technique it invented, Convar has recovered data from computers damaged by fire, dust, or water during the September 11, 2001, attacks on New York City's World Trade Center.

CHAPTER | THREE

COMPUTER FORENSICS

▼ **COMPUTER FORENSICS, SOMETIMES** called digital forensics or electronic evidence recovery, is one of the newer branches of forensic science. It consists of examining computers and related media, such as disks and storage drives, to find and analyze data that may serve as evidence in a legal or criminal case. The data may be photos, videos, e-mails, music files, text files (documents), or the locations of Web sites that a given user has visited.

One of the computer forensic specialist's most important tasks is to find and preserve "hidden" data. Many computer users may be surprised to learn that information that they never intentionally saved, or that they had deleted long ago, still exists on their hard drives, even though it does not show up on the computer's directory of files. Until this old or deleted data has been overwritten by new programs or files that the user creates, it can be recovered through forensic techniques. Although data that has been overwritten is not

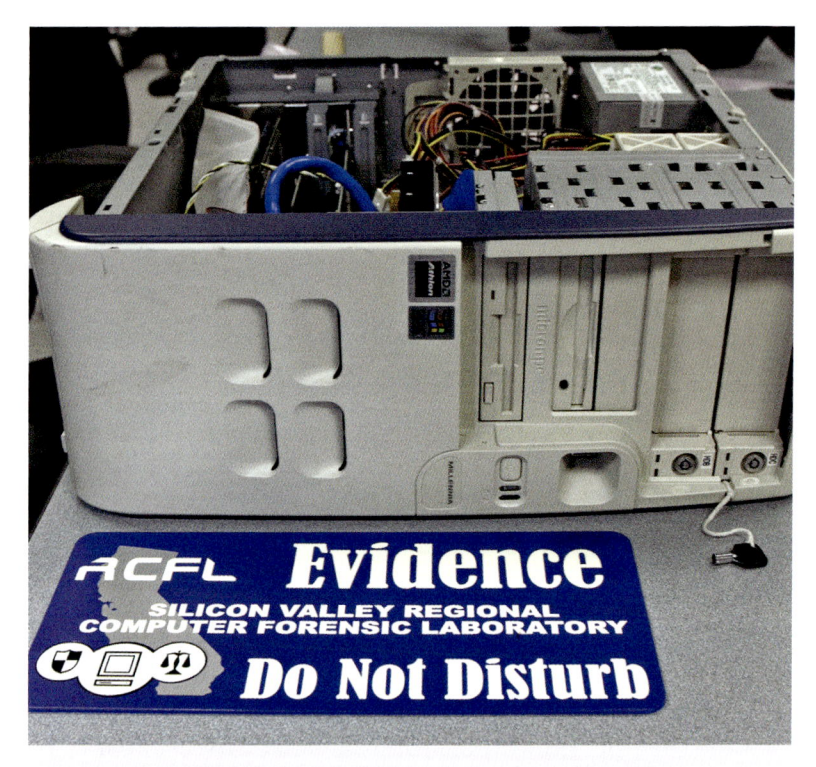

▲ A computer lies open for evidence recovery at the Silicon Valley Regional Computer Forensic Laboratory. The facility, which opened in 2005, is part of a network of fourteen such labs that operate in partnership with local law enforcement and the FBI.

recoverable, even computers with full hard drives have many small pockets of unused space that contain pieces of old data. Forensic specialists can usually recover much of this buried material. Hidden information may also include files or programs that the user has protected with passwords, as well as data that has been encrypted, or converted into a code or cipher.

Like other forensic specialties, computer forensics calls for special training and equipment—resources that not every law enforcement agency can afford. As a result, although agencies such as the FBI and some large police departments have full-time digital forensic specialists or even whole departments, many police and sheriff's departments rely on outside experts who work on digital forensics cases as needed. Prosecutors, who are the lawyers who represent the state in cases against people accused of committing crimes, frequently call upon such specialists to serve as expert witnesses during trials. So do defense attorneys, the lawyers who defend the accused.

A good forensic specialist not only analyzes the digital evidence but also is able to explain his or her procedures and findings clearly to judges, attorneys, and jurors. This is no simple task, because the evidence in digital forensics cases is often highly technical, full of terms and concepts that are unfamiliar to the general public.

▶ GUIDELINES FOR COMPUTER CRIME INVESTIGATORS

Investigators in any case involving computer forensics should follow three universal guidelines. First, they must do nothing to alter the original digital materials that are being examined. This means that the experts must perform all their work on exact images, or copies, of hard drives and disks, never on the actual drives and disks. The investigation of the data takes place not on the seized computers but on other computers that read the images. The use of imaged, or copied, data is necessary for several reasons. No investigator wants to face the consequences of losing or damaging digital material, whether that material turns out to be evidence of guilt or the legal private property of a computer's owner. In addition, unless the original is maintained in an untouched state that can later be verified, defense attorneys can suggest that the evidence may have been altered, even tampered with, during the investigation.

The second guideline is that each stage of the investigation should be thoroughly documented, ideally in more than one medium. For example, if police obtain a search warrant that gives them the authority to seize and examine someone's computer, the documentation might begin with photographs, sketches, and, if possible, videotape of the room housing the computer in question as well as the search process. Documentation should show the exact position of such features as power outlets, keyboards, telephones, disks, and computers themselves, as well as the cables and cords connecting them.

Documentation should cover the make and model of each piece of equipment. It should also show the condition of the equipment, especially any signs of damage that are visible before the investigation begins. As the investigation continues, the forensic specialist should keep a careful record of every action performed on the computer or its data. Some forensic software tools produce their own records, but analysts should still maintain logs of what they do, when they do it, and what results they obtain.

Documentation is closely related to the third guideline, which is that investigators must maintain an unbroken chain of custody. The chain-of-custody principle applies to all forensic evidence, not just to digital materials. It means that every piece of evidence should be accounted for at all times, whether it is stored in an evidence locker, being analyzed in a lab, being exhibited in court, or in transit from one place to another. In practice, maintaining the chain of custody simply means that every time the evidence

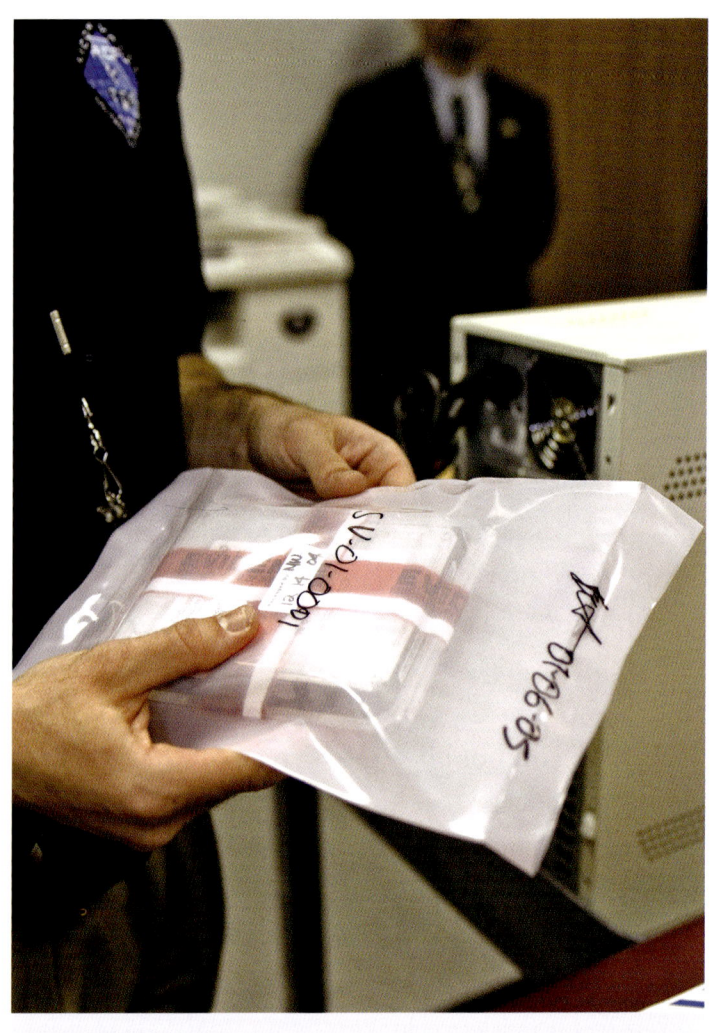

▲ Bagged and tagged as evidence, the hard drive from a seized computer is protected from damage to the data it contains. Cyber forensic specialists must master not only computer skills but also the rules of proper evidence handling.

changes hands, the person handing it over, as well as the person who takes charge of it, must sign it (or an attached form), giving the date and time the evidence was handed off or received. If the chain of custody remains unbroken, it is clear who was responsible for the evidence at each stage, with no gaps. A broken chain of custody raises the possibility of mishandling or tampering. This may mean that prosecutors cannot use that evidence in their case.

When the evidence consists of digital material, forensic specialists can use hash codes as part of the documentation of the chain of custody. A hash code is a number, the result of an automatic mathematical calculation, that the computer applies to each drive and each file on the drive. Whenever any change is made to a drive or a file, its hash code changes. Digital forensic specialists can check and record the hash codes of the original evidence and the images of it at various stages of the investigation. Hash codes that remain unchanged show that the investigators have not altered the underlying data in any way.

▶ DIGITAL FORENSIC PROCEDURES

Every case is different, but certain basic procedures apply to all cases of computer-related crime, even if the person who handles the digital materials is not a computer forensic specialist. Many police and sheriff's departments have provided their nonspecialist officers with training or guidelines to handle computer-related evidence.

SEARCHING THE SCENE

Investigators must pay attention to everything at the scene of a search, not just the computers. Many computer users store useful information such as passwords on pieces of paper taped to the side of the monitor or the underside of the keyboard. Investigators have also located computer disks, password lists, and other helpful items concealed inside books, CD cases, and other objects.

SECURING EVIDENCE

Crime scene specialists sometimes call the process of collecting and securing evidence "bagging and tagging." It may seem that computer hardware would be easy to bag (or box) and tag with identifying labels, but securing digital evidence can be a dramatic process.

A computer owner with something to hide may try to destroy the evidence as soon as he or she realizes that the police are knocking on the door—or, in cases of serious crimes, breaking it down. The user may press a key that activates a "wipe" program. Such programs, which are both commercially available and custom-built, are designed to instantly erase data. Often they do

COMPUTER FORENSICS

not work as well as the user expects them to, but they make the forensic investigator's job more difficult.

A suspect may also try to destroy evidence with a magnet (magnetic fields scramble data) or with cruder tools. Officers have found computers smashed with axes and cement blocks. Panicked suspects have even fired

▲ A crime scene officer removes a computer, wrapped to preserve fingerprints, for forensic examination. A crime scene suit prevents the officer from contaminating the scene with hair, fingerprints, or other trace evidence that could mislead investigators.

guns at their hard drives in the hope of destroying evidence. Again, while such physical damage may not prevent all data from being recovered, it makes the task a lot harder. Investigators should enter the scene as quickly as possible. Once they are on the scene, it is important that they keep everyone who is not on the investigative team away from the equipment.

MAKING THE IMAGE

Before the physical evidence is moved, all suspected computer drives should be imaged, or copied in exact detail. If possible, this should be done before the computer is turned off or disconnected from its power source, because every action taken on a computer, even something as simple as turning the machine on or off, causes automatic changes to the files stored on the drives. Although such changes are invisible to the ordinary computer user, they can overwrite or otherwise affect hidden data that might serve as evidence.

The images should be made on clean, virus-protected media such as hard drives, zip disks, or writable CD or DVD disks. All such media should be equipped with write-blocking software. This prevents anyone from writing new data onto the media, which means that defense attorneys will not be able to claim that the data on an image that is presented as evidence was tampered with or contaminated.

Before packing up the evidence for transport to a police station, laboratory, or evidence locker, the investigators should verify that they have indeed captured images of all drives and files, and that the captured files are readable. Although a forensic examiner can perform the imaging and the verification manually by clicking on drive directories and file names, most specialists use software programs that perform both functions.

PROTECTING EVIDENCE

When possible, police departments and other law enforcement agencies should store computers and related objects in evidence rooms that have been specially designed or arranged for such materials. Computer evidence should be stored away from direct sunlight, at temperatures between 60 and 90 degrees Fahrenheit. It should not be stored on carpeting or plastic shelving, which can cause static electricity. A dust-free environment is desirable. There should be no magnetic fields, even the weak ones created by radios or refrigerator magnets. (These are good tips for ordinary computer owners, too.)

RECOVERING DATA

The evidence that a digital forensic specialist analyzes is not the suspect's computer but the images made of the computer's drives. As the first step in the analysis, the forensic specialist surveys the contents of each drive, looking for hidden, invisible, erased, and deleted files as well as visible ones that appear to be relevant to the case. The examiner also searches for partitioned drives, which are sections of the hard drive that have been set aside as hidden drives or vaults. Forensic examiners typically use software programs designed to scan drives and reveal the presence of partitions and hidden files.

The next step is to use other software programs to recover deleted and erased data. Some of these programs are widely available utilities that are prepackaged with operating systems. Others are more sophisticated, designed specifically for forensic use. Many of these programs operate automatically once they are installed, but examiners can also scan and recover data manually by entering commands into the operating system.

DECRYPTING FILES

Examiners may be prompted to enter passwords at various stages of their analysis. Some computer users employ passwords to prevent unauthorized users from starting up their computers. In such cases, while anyone can turn the power on, the computer will not boot up (its operating system will not start) until the boot password, also called the CMOS password, is entered.

When confronted with a computer that will not start without a boot password and a suspect who refuses to reveal the password, investigators have several options. Depending upon the type of computer hardware involved, they may be able to bypass the CMOS password by opening the computer, removing the motherboard (a flat platform that holds the chips and circuits that operate the computer), and physically manipulating the chips, circuits, or batteries. These operations require care and experience, however, as exposing the motherboard risks damaging the computer hardware or data. Another possibility is a

▲ Most computer users create passwords for certain purposes. Hackers sometimes "crack" passwords by using knowledge or guesswork about a victim's nickname, hobbies, birth date, pet's name, and so on—a technique that hackers call "social engineering."

backdoor or default password. Some computer and chip manufacturers build these defaults—passwords that can be used by anyone—into their products. Defaults are available from the manufacturer or even online.

Investigators may also try to guess the password, or at least to come up with a list of possibilities, based on what they know about a suspect. Many people use guessable passwords such as the names of pets or loved ones, birthdays, their own names spelled backward, and so on. If all else fails, investigators may be desperate enough to resort to the time-consuming and often ineffective tactic hackers call "brute force": trying combination after combination in the hope that one will work.

Once they get past the CMOS password, examiners may find that the user has applied other passwords to particular programs, files, or documents. A file that is password-protected has been encrypted, or converted into a coded form called a cipher that hides its content. File encryption is based on the ancient art and science of cryptography, the study of ciphers. An encrypted file can be compared to an egg that has been scrambled. All the original material is present, but in unrecognizable form. Although an egg cannot be unscrambled, an encrypted message can be **decrypted**—that is, converted into readable form—but only if the key to the cipher is available. In the case of password protection, the key is the password.

The most direct way to get a password is to ask the computer user who created it. If the user refuses to reveal the password, or if the user cannot be found, investigators can try using software programs called password crackers. These are most likely to work on the fairly simple encryption programs that come prepackaged with many varieties of consumer software, such as Microsoft Word and Excel. Users who are interested in a higher level of security, however, may have purchased or downloaded stronger encryption programs that are very difficult, sometimes impossible, to crack, even for advanced cracking programs.

One way to crack a strong encryption program is to capture the password *before* the suspect is aware of the investigation. In some cases investigators have focused hidden cameras on suspects' keyboards to film the suspects as they typed in their secret passwords. More often, however, investigators gain access to the suspect's computer and install a keystroke logger without the suspect's knowledge. The logger can be either a small piece of hardware or a software program; either way, it records everything that is typed on a computer's keyboard, including passwords. Such methods can be used only when the evidence against the suspect is strong enough that investigators can obtain warrants for data tapping. One such case in 2002 involved Nicodemus Scarfo Jr., the son of a New Jersey crime boss. The FBI used a keystroke logger to obtain Scarfo's password, then used the password to decrypt files that contained records of illegal gambling.

EXAMINING EVIDENCE

The final step in data analysis is to look at the contents of recovered files. In many cases, however, investigators cannot simply look at every file on a given computer. A search warrant that allows authorities to seize a computer usually specifies the particular crime that is being investigated and the kinds of evidence that may be examined. In a case of suspected child pornography, for example, investigators may be allowed to view only pictures, along with documents and e-mails that appear to contain evidence of the crime. The suspect's other files, such as financial information and personal correspondence, are not part of the evidence. Examiners should also check for the presence of Trojan horses and viruses in a suspect's drives, because the suspect may claim that incriminating files were carried into his computer, without his knowledge, by malware.

When the examination is complete and all useful evidence has been copied and documented, investigators must usually return the computer and its contents to the owner (unless the owner is in prison). Computers are so central to life today that the courts have repeatedly ruled that depriving individuals, families, and businesses of access to them is an unacceptable hardship. Authorities are expected to remove all illegal or stolen material from a confiscated computer before returning it, however.

▶ THE PASSWORD PROBLEM

Encryption software is a controversial subject. From the point of view of civil liberties activists such as the Electronic Frontier Foundation (EFF), an organization dedicated to preserving individual liberties in the digital era, every citizen has the right to protect his or her information. Encryption, in this view, is a valuable tool for preventing identity theft and preserving freedom of speech. From the point of view of law enforcement, however, encryption is an unwelcome obstacle. Its benefits to criminals are believed to outweigh its usefulness to ordinary citizens.

The conflict over encryption centers on powerful programs such as Pretty Good Privacy (PGP), which was introduced in 1991. When copies of PGP made their way outside the United States two years later, the U.S. government charged the program's creator with exporting

▲ Phil Zimmerman created Pretty Good Privacy (PGP), an encryption program so powerful that the U.S. government once considered it a potential weapon. Today the widespread use of PGP and similar programs raises questions of individual rights versus law enforcement.

munitions, or weaponry, without a license. The program was so powerful that it could be classified as a military material. The charges were eventually dropped, however, and PGP went on to become widely available.

Although files encrypted with PGP have been cracked through luck and persistent brute force attacks, many cryptographers consider the program to be uncrackable by code-breaking programs or formulas. In a case that is now making its way through the court system, a U.S. Secret Service expert in computer security testified that the only way to get at PGP-protected data without the password would be to use an automated guessing program that might take years to hit the right combination.

The controversial case started in December 2006 when Sebastian Boucher, a Canadian citizen who is a legal resident of New Hampshire, tried to cross from Canada into the United States with his laptop computer. During a routine check, and with Boucher's cooperation, border officials scanned the computer's file directory. Some of the file names they saw suggested that the computer contained child pornography. The agents then looked at some of those files; later they described them as containing illegal images. Boucher, who said that he downloaded adult pornography but sometimes received child pornography without knowing it or intending to receive it, was arrested. Authorities seized his laptop but could not search one drive, which was protected by PGP. Boucher had opened the drive for the border officials, but the computer had been turned off after the initial inspection. Without Boucher's password authorities could not reopen the drive.

A grand jury issued a subpoena to try to force Boucher to reveal the password, but in late 2007 a federal magistrate ruled that the subpoena cannot be enforced. According to the magistrate, Boucher's password is protected under the Fifth Amendment to the Constitution, which guarantees that no one can be forced to incriminate himself or herself. The government has appealed this ruling to a higher court. For now the question remains: Do people have the right to keep their passwords secret?

▶ WHO USES DIGITAL FORENSICS?

Criminal investigation is not the only use for computer forensics. People use the tools and techniques of digital forensics in a variety of other situations. Computer forensics experts may be called upon to secure evidence in civil cases such as divorces, insurance claims, or lawsuits for damages. Some corporations or businesses employ IT professionals, or hire outside experts, to review their computer security procedures and to monitor internal operations such as bookkeeping for signs of possible wrongdoing. In addition, corporations often carry out their own internal investigations of matters such as hacking or industrial espionage, which is the theft of valuable business information, including marketing plans and product designs, by competing businesses.

The tools of computer forensics also have a place in everyday life. Technicians at computer repair services are often called upon to recover data that people have lost because of hard drive crashes, damage to their computers, or overenthusiastic deleting. If you have ever mistakenly deleted a file and then figured out how to "undelete" it, perhaps by using the help guide in your software program, you have performed a limited version of what computer forensic experts do.

According to a report issued in 2007 by the FBI and the Internet Crime Complaint Center (IC3), the IC3 received nearly 207,500 complaints about Internet crimes in 2006—a decrease of more than 10 percent from 2005. Perhaps the decrease is an encouraging sign that Internet crime is down, or that people are becoming more careful users of the Internet. On the other hand, the amount of money lost to fraud and other Internet crimes rose from $183 million in 2005 to more than $198 million in 2006, which may mean that cybercrime is becoming more profitable. In any case, cybercrime will probably endure for as long as people continue to use computers and the Internet—and so will computer forensics.

Protect Your Computer from Cybercrooks

IN A WORLD FULL of black hats and worms, crackers and Trojan horses, how can you ensure the safety of your computer, your gateway to cyberspace? The FBI's Cyber Operations division recommends these basic steps:

1. **Use a firewall.**
This piece of software or hardware is designed to keep hackers or automated hacking programs called bots from gaining access to your computer. Firewalls are prepackaged with the operating systems of many computers—some versions of Windows, for example, contain firewalls. If your computer does not have a firewall, or if you want a stronger one than the manufacturer provided, many choices are available. Purchase or download your firewall only from a reliable, trusted source. Once you have installed your firewall, keep it turned on. A firewall is especially important if you use a wireless Internet connection, which puts your computer at greater risk of being hacked than a wired connection does.

2. **Use antivirus software.**
Antivirus programs scan incoming material for viruses, worms, and Trojan horses. They block infected material from entering and also scan

Cyberspace can be dangerous, but you can take steps to protect your data and keep your computer, and your Internet experience, safe.

your computer's hard drive and files for any harmful code that might have slipped in. It is not enough simply to install or activate an antivirus program. You must also update it every time the manufacturer of the program issues protections against new viruses and worms. Most antivirus programs can be set to update themselves automatically when you go online. Although the vast majority of viruses and worms target Microsoft Windows, the most widely used computer operating system in the world, malware has been created to infect the other operating systems, too.

3. **Consider antispyware protection.**
Spyware consists of programs that enter your computer from sites you visit. Sometimes spyware enters your computer along with something you have downloaded. It may produce unwanted

ads on your computer or collect information about your online buying or viewing habits and send that information to marketers who will target you with ads. Like firewalls, antispyware technology is prepackaged with some computer operating systems. It is also available commercially. Like antivirus software, it should be kept up to date.

4. **Update your operating system regularly**.
Every operating system—Windows, Mac, Linux, and the others—is updated by its manufacturer or developer from time to time. Updates often patch security holes that have been found to be vulnerable to hackers or malware. You can find information about how to update safely and regularly in your operating system's help file.

5. **Download wisely**.
When you download files or open e-mail attachments, you risk introducing a virus or worm that is so new that antivirus protection is not yet in place. Never open an e-mail attachment from someone you don't know. Be wary of forwarded attachments even if they come from someone you know. By passing on jokes, cartoons, photos, and other items, people have unknowingly passed viruses and worms to their friends, family members, and coworkers. If you receive an attachment you're not sure about, wait a few days and update your antivirus protection before opening it. Better yet, when in doubt, delete.

6. **Turn off your Internet connection when you are not online.**
You may think that it is convenient to keep your Internet connection always open and ready to use, but this practice leaves your computer needlessly vulnerable. The strongest protection against attack is the off switch.

Your most valuable piece of protective software is your own common sense. Use caution when navigating cyberspace, where things and people are not always what they appear to be. Social networking sites, online multiplayer games, and other locations that appeal to young people also appeal to criminals who target the young. Never share with strangers any information that could be used to identify you or your family. If you experience harassment or unwanted attention online, report it to the site's administrator.

If a skilled hacker is determined to break down your computer's defenses, no matter how much time and effort it takes, he or she will probably succeed. Fortunately, ordinary citizens rarely become targets of such focused attacks. In general, household and student computers are at much greater risk from viruses, worms, and spyware than from master hackers. Although perfect protection is never guaranteed, the steps listed here will protect most computers from most threats.

・・・・・

▼ GLOSSARY

computer forensics tools and techniques that investigators use to gather and examine evidence of cybercrimes; specifically, the handling of computer drives and data in the course of an investigation

cracker a malicious hacker who intends to cause harm; sometimes called a black hat

cybercrime an illegal activity that targets a computer or uses a computer as the means of committing a crime; also called computer crime

decrypt to decode a cipher text, or encrypted text

digital based on converting information, including text, pictures, and sounds, into streams of binary digits, represented by combinations of 1s and 0s; computers use and transmit data in digital form

encrypt to turn a text into a cipher text, or coded text, usually done with software programs

forensic science the use of scientific knowledge or methods to investigate crimes, identify suspects, and try criminal cases in court

forensics in general, debate or review of any question of fact relating to the law; often used to refer to forensic science

hacker someone who gains (or tries to gain) unauthorized access to a computer or a computer network

malware malicious or harmful forms of software, including viruses, worms, and Trojan horses

phishing trying to get confidential information, such as passwords or credit card numbers, through a fraudulent e-mail message that tricks the recipient into releasing the information, usually by pretending to be from a trusted source such as a bank or major corporation

phreaker someone who hacks or breaks into telecommunications systems, such as telephone lines, usually to make free calls

spam unwanted junk e-mail, usually sent to millions of people, often a means of spreading viruses or worms

Trojan horse software program that pretends to be something it is not so that users will accept it into their systems and activate it

virus software program that reproduces itself inside computer systems and spreads by concealing itself in disks, files, or documents, which are then considered to be infected

worm software program that reproduces itself inside computer systems; it can spread from one system to another without being concealed in a document, file, or disk

▼ FIND OUT MORE

FURTHER READING

Blane, John V. *Cybercrime and Cyberterrorism.* New York: Novinka Books, 2003.

Funkhluser, John. *Forensic Science for High School Students.* Dubuque, IA: Kendall Hunt, 2005.

Mattern, Joanne. *Forensics.* San Diego, CA: Blackbirch Press, 2004.

Moore, Robert. *Cybercrime: Investigating High-Technology Computer Crime.* Student edition. Cincinnati, OH: Anderson, 2005.

Newman, Matthew. *You Have Mail: True Stories of Cybercrime.* New York and London: Franklin Watts, 2007.

Owen, David. *Police Lab: How Forensic Science Tracks Down and Convicts Criminals.* Toronto: Firefly, 2002.

Platt, Richard. *Crime Scene: The Ultimate Guide to Forensic Science.* New York: Dorling Kindersley, 2003.

WEB SITES

www.aafs.org/yfsf/index.htm

The Web site of the American Academy of Forensic Sciences features the Young Forensic Scientists Forum, with information on careers in forensics. The site also has links to other Internet resources.

www.computerforensicsworld.com/

Computer Forensics World is a site for and about people who

work in the digital forensics industry, as well as those who are interested in computer crime and forensics.

www.courttv.com/forensics_curriculum/
Developed by CourtTV (now truTV), the American Academy of Forensic Sciences, and the National Science Teachers Association, this kid-friendly Forensics in the Classroom site introduces forensic science with a glossary, timeline, and virtual forensics lab.

www.cybercrime.gov/
The Computer Crime and Intellectual Property section of the Department of Justice's Web site contains links to hundreds of articles about computer crime and the law.

www.eff.org
The Electronic Frontier Foundation, dedicated to protecting individual and civil rights in the digital world, has articles on cybercrime and computer-related legislation and law enforcement.

www.fbi.gov/cyberinvest/cyberhome.htm
The Web site of the Federal Bureau of Investigation (FBI) offers this section on cyber investigations, with definitions, statistics, case histories, and links to other resources.

www.forensicfocus.com

The Forensic Focus site contains news and information about computer forensics; the site is aimed at digital forensic specialists but contains articles and information for law enforcement and the general public as well, including details about training for a career in digital forensics.

www.forensicmag.com/

Forensic Magazine's Web page features case studies and news about developments in criminalistics and other branches of forensic science.

http://law.udayton.edu/cybercrimes/

The University of Dayton School of Law maintains this cybercrimes page, with articles about legal and forensic issues as well as news stories about computer crimes.

www.lib.msu.edu/harris23/crimjust/cybercri.htm

Michigan State University maintains this site devoted to computer crime, with links to other university and government sites.

http://onguardonline.gov/index.html

Half a dozen U.S. government agencies cooperate to sponsor the OnGuard Online site, which tells computer users how to protect themselves from Internet fraud and identity theft.

▼ BIBLIOGRAPHY

The author found these resources especially helpful when researching this book.

Baggili, Ibrahim, and Matthew Kiley. "Digital Forensics: A Brief Overview of Critical Issues." *Forensic Magazine*, October/November 2007, online at http://www.forensicmag.com/articles.asp?pid=170

Biggs, John. *Black Hat: Misfits, Criminals, and Scammers in the Internet Age.* Berkeley, CA: Apress, 2004.

Blitstein, Ryan. "Ghosts in the Browser." *San Jose Mercury News*, November 9–13, 2007, online at http://www.siliconvalley.com/ghostsinthebrowser

Branigan, Steven. *High-Tech Crimes Revealed: Cyberwar Stories from the Digital Front.* Boston: Addison-Wesley, 2005.

Britz, Marjie T. *Computer Forensics and Cyber Crime: An Introduction.* Upper Saddle River, NJ: Pearson, 2004.

Furnell, Steven. *Cybercrime: Vandalizing the Information Society.* Boston: Addison-Wesley, 2002.

Ramsland, Katherine. *The C.S.I. Effect.* New York: Berkley, 2006.

Rhoads, Chris. "The Twilight Years of Cap'n Crunch." *Wall Street Journal*, January 13, 2007, online at http://online.wsj.com/public/article/SB116863379291775523_EQCu93LyjSommsN6J7qiCozuu8_20070122.html?mod=blogs

Saferstein, Richard. *Criminalistics: An Introduction to Forensic Science.* Upper Saddle River, NJ: Prentice Hall, 2003.

▼ INDEX

Page numbers in **boldface** are illustrations, tables, and charts.

antispyware protection, 83–84
antivirus software, **53**, 82–83, 84
ARPANET, 48

backdoor, 58, 74
"bagging and tagging", **66**, 68–70
ballistics, 10
black hat hackers, 33, 82
blue boxes, 16–18, 20–21
bot, 58, 82
botnet, 58–59
Boucher, Sebastian, 79
Britz, Marjie T., 35
"brute force", 74, 78–79

call-center service, 43
Cantrell, Calvin, 22, 23, 26
Captain Crunch, 20–21, **21**
chain-of-custody, 65, 67
child pornography, 41, 76, 79
cipher, 74, 75
civil liberties, 77
CMOS password, 72–74
Computer Emergency Response Team (CERT), 56
computer forensics, 6, 13, 36, 59, 63, 86
 guidelines for, 64–67
 uses for, 80–81
Computer Fraud and Abuse Act (CFAA), 56
computer protection, 82–83

computers
 as crime targets, 35, 43–49
 as crime tools, 35, 36–43
 incidental to crime, 35–36
cracker, 30, 82, 86
criminalistics, 11
cryptography, 74, 79
cybercrime, 5–6, 11, 22, 59, 86
 categories, 35, 36–49
 profitability, 81
cyberextortion, 40–41
cyberstalking, 36–37
Cyber Storm, 50, 51
cyberterrorism, 49–53

data recovery, **60**, 61–63, 71–72, 76, 81
data tapping, 23–26, 76
decrypt, 72–76, 86
default password, 74
DEF CON event, 31, **32**
deleted data, 72, 81
denial of service (DoS) attack, 45, 46, 47
digital, 23, 27, 42, 64, 67–68, 77, 86
digital forensics, 60, 63
 procedures, 67–77
 uses for, 80–81
documentation, 64–65, 76
Donahue, Tom, 49, 50
Draper, John, 20–21, **21**

embezzlement, 39, 40
encrypt, 63, 74–75, 77–78, 86
evidence protection, **69**, 71
extortion, 40–41

firewall, 82
forensic manuals, 8, 10–11
forensic science, 6, 8, 86
forensics, 7, 8, 13, 86
419 scheme, 38

gray hats, 33
the Great Worm, 55–56
Gross, Hans, 10–11

hack attacks, 44–47, 51, 53
hacker, 15–16, 21–22, 25–28, 36, 40–41, 57–59, 80, 86
  historic, 47–49
  image, 27–28, 49
  protection against, 82, 84–85
  tactics, 74
  vocabulary, 30–33
hacktivists, 30
hash code, 67

identity theft, 6, 26, 36, 39, 77
imaged/copied data, 64, 70–71, 76
in-band signaling, 16
industrial espionage, 80
Internet Filter Review, 41

keystroke logger, 75, 76

Legion of Doom, 19, 27
Lindsly, Corey, 22, 26
logic bomb, 59

Mafiaboy, 45–46
magnetic fields scramble data, 69, 71

malware, 53–59, 76, 83–84, 86
Mitnick, Kevin, 47, 48, **48**, 49
Morris, Michael, 22, 23
Morris, Robert Tappan, 55–56, **57**
motherboard, 73
multifrequency tone generator, 17, 18

Napster, 42, 43
National Cyber Security Division (NCSD), 50, 53
Nigerian fee scheme, 38
Nugache worm, 58

Orfila, Mathieu, 9
organized crime syndicate, 59

Paller, Alan, 41
partitioned drives, 72
passwords, 72–76, **73**, 79
phishing, 39, 87
Phonemasters, 22–23, 25–27
phreaker, 15–22, 27, 87
piracy, 42, 44, 49
Pretty Good Privacy (PGP), 77–79, **78**

salami scheme, 40
Scarfo, Nicodemus Jr., 76
scene of a search, 68
script kiddies, 30
sneakers, 30
software piracy, 44, 49
spam, 37–38, 57–58, 87
speech, freedom of, 77
spyware, 83, 85

Storm worm, 57, 58, 59

tampered evidence, 67, 70
telephone system, 16–18, **17**, 23, **24**, 25, 27
time bomb, 59
Trojan horse, 58, 76, 82, 87
trolling, 41

U.S. Air Force Cyber Command (AFCYBER), 52
U.S. Computer Emergency Readiness Team (US-CERT), 56

virus, 6, 13, 54, 56–57, 59, 76, 82–85, 87

wares dudes, 30
Web War I, 46–47
white hats, 31
"wipe" program, 68
Wood, Tom, 31, 32
worm, 6, **7**, 54–59, **55**, 82–85, 87
Wynne, Michael, 52

▼ ABOUT THE AUTHOR

REBECCA STEFOFF has written many books on scientific subjects for young readers. She has explored the world of evolutionary biology in Marshall Cavendish's Family Trees series; she also wrote *Microscopes and Telescopes* and *The Camera* for the same publisher's Great Inventions series. After publishing *Charles Darwin and the Evolution Revolution* (Oxford University Press, 1996), Stefoff appeared in the *A&E Biography* program on Darwin and his work. She lives in Portland, Oregon. You can learn more about her books for young readers at **www.rebeccastefoff.com**.